MUM JOKES

MUM JOKES

Over 500 of the world's greatest, eye-rolling, family-friendly, funny jokes

JESSICA ROWE

MUM, PODCASTER, TIKTOKKER, PROUD CRAP HOUSEWIFE

ALLEN&UNWIN
SYDNEY • MELBOURNE • AUCKLAND • LONDON

Allen & Unwin
Cammeraygal Country
83 Alexander Street
Crows Nest NSW 2065
Australia
Phone: (61 2) 8425 0100
Email: info@allenandunwin.com
Web: www.allenandunwin.com

*Allen & Unwin acknowledges the Traditional Owners of the Country on which we
live and work. We pay our respects to all Aboriginal and Torres Strait Islander
Elders, past and present.*

A catalogue record for this
book is available from the
National Library of Australia

ISBN 978 1 76106 873 7

Illustration and Text Design by Louisa Maggio Design
Set in Harriet Text by Post Pre-press Group, Brisbane
Printed and bound in Australia by the Opus Group

10 9 8 7 6 5 4 3 2 1

The paper in this book is FSC® certified.
FSC® promotes environmentally responsible,
socially beneficial and economically viable
management of the world's forests.

For my girls and Petee!

I'm so lucky to have you

A good laugh is sunshine in the house.

William Thackeray

Why Mum Jokes?

I crack myself up. All the time. Even if my teenage daughters roll their eyes in embarrassment and my husband tells me, 'That is SO not funny!'

Thankfully my friends (well, some of them) think I'm hilarious. Oh, it's life-affirming and essential to surround yourself with people who make you laugh and also laugh with you.

I haven't always been a confident joke teller. Why? Well, I'm a shocker at telling longer jokes, as I lose my way and I frequently forget the punchline.

Once on live television I decided it was time to face my fear. I had my bestie Denise Drysdale, who is comedy treasure, sitting next to me, and she promised to step in if it looked like I was losing the audience.

My heart was beating fast and my hands were clammy. The camera came in for a close-up . . . and Neesy had to bolt to the bathroom! Thanks for that. There I was left in the lurch, in joke limbo. I fumbled my way through the joke and this time I had to agree with my husband Petee: it wasn't funny.

However, I'm not one to ever give up when I'm passionate about something. Laughing is what I love to do. So I went searching for short jokes that were easy to remember and that I found funny. This collection of mum jokes is the result of that search. I hope that they will make you laugh too.

Often I like to team my jokes with a matching outfit or a specially crafted hat for maximum impact. But this collection stands alone if you want to stay dressed down while you share them with your loved ones.

Let's hear it for the mum joke! No more boring dad jokes. It's time for us marvellous, funny, wise, quirky women to claim our place in joke history. And look out, comedy stages—I'm coming for you next.

You can imagine how thrilled my daughters are about that.

Follow my joke-telling adventures on Instagram @jessjrowe or on TikTok @craphousewife.

Jess Rowe

When women reach
a certain age they start
accumulating cats.

This is known
as many paws.

I just saw a car being
driven by a sheep
in a swimsuit . . .

It was a lamb bikini.

What's the difference between
black-eyed peas and chickpeas?

Black-eyed peas can actually sing us a song.
Chickpeas can only hummus one.

What kind of music do
mummies listen to?

Wrap music.

What do you call
a pile of pussycats?

A meow-tain.

What do you call
a fake noodle?

An impasta.

I asked if I could have some peace
and quiet while I cooked dinner.

So my teenage daughters took the
battery out of the smoke alarm.

What do you call a fox with
a carrot in its ear?

Anything! Because
it can't hear you.

How do you count cows?

With a cow-culator!

What did the baby corn say
to the mama corn?

'Where's Pop-corn?'

What do you get when you cross
a hamburger with a computer?

A Big Mac!

How can you spot
a fashionista donut?

It's in all the latest glazes.

All mum jokes
must be written down
on a piece of paper.

It's not a mum joke
unless it's tearable.

Where do spaghetti
and sauce go to dance?

The meat ball.

What singers do bees love?

Bee-yoncé, Sting, Bee-thoven, the Bee-tales, Justin Bee-ber and the Bee Gees.

Why did the fungi leave the party?

There wasn't mushroom.

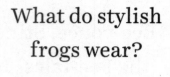

What do stylish
frogs wear?

Jumpsuits.

What do you get
if you put hot water
down a rabbit hole?

Hot cross bunny.

Mr Bigger and Mrs Bigger
had a baby.
Who's the biggest in the family?

The baby—she's a little Bigger.

What do you call a cheese
that isn't yours?

Na-cho cheese.

What do you call a fish
with no eye?

A fshhhhhh.

I used to be addicted to
the hokey-pokey.

And then I turned
myself around.

Why did the chicken
cross the road?

The chicken next
to him farted.

What kind of chocolate
do you find in the fluff-catching
drawer of the dryer?

Lindt.

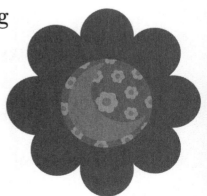

What do you call a dinosaur
with no eyes?

I-don't-think-he-saw-us.

How do you make a tissue dance?

Put a little boogie in it.

How does a banana
answer the phone?

Yellow!

Guess who I bumped into on my
way to get my glasses fixed?

Everybody!

How do you get clean
in outer space?

You take a meteor shower.

Why do cats
make dodgy DJs?

They always paws
the tunes.

What do you call a chook
looking at a lettuce?

Chicken sees a salad.

I have named
my horse Mayo.

And occasionally
Mayo neighs.

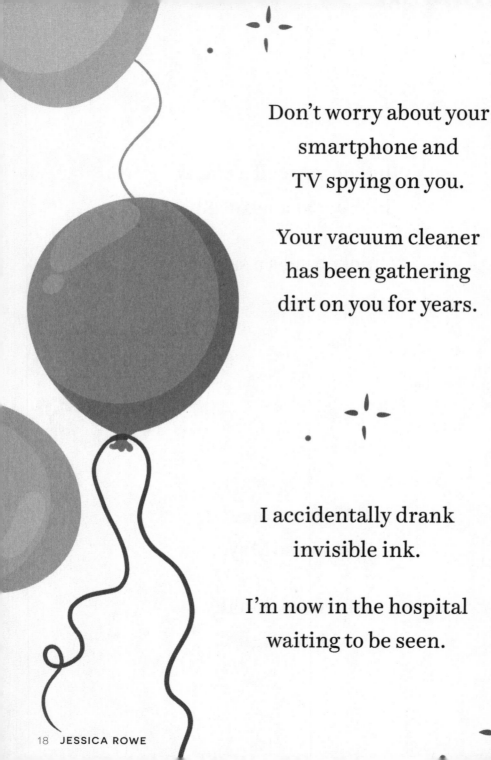

Don't worry about your
smartphone and
TV spying on you.

Your vacuum cleaner
has been gathering
dirt on you for years.

I accidentally drank
invisible ink.

I'm now in the hospital
waiting to be seen.

What happens when
you cross an angry sheep
and an angry cow?

You get two animals
in a *baaad moood*.

I quit my job at the
helium factory today.

I refuse to be spoken to
in that tone.

A donut, a cupcake and an
ice-cream cone crossed the road.

The streets were oddly
desserted that night.

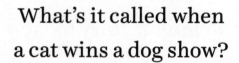

What's it called when
a cat wins a dog show?

A cat-has-trophy.

What do you call a man
who just got botox
on his mouth?

Phil-lip.

How do you cheer up a fox
who lost its tail?

By sending it on some
re-tail therapy.

What did the shark say after
eating a clown fish?

'You taste a little funny.'

Why are pirates
called pirates?

Because they arrrgh!!!

What do you call a tortoise
with balance issues?

Tortellini.

Did you hear Elton John
bought a treadmill
for his pet rabbit?

It's a little fit bunny . . .

Why do ants never get sick?

Because they have
little anty bodies.

A lion, a witch and a wardrobe enter a bar;
the bartender looks at them suspiciously
and asks, 'What are you up to?'

The lion responds gruffly,
'Narnia business!'

Did you hear about the cat
who drank five bowls
of water?

He set a new lap record.

What did the mummy spider
say to the baby spider?

'You spend too much time
on the web.'

Did anyone go to
the donut party?

I hear it was
jam packed!

What is a kitten's favourite
kitchen accessory?

A whisk-er!

What is a koala's favourite
Christmas carol?

Deck the halls with boughs of holly.
Koala la la la la la la laaaaa.

Why shouldn't you take
a bear to the zoo?

Because they'd rather
go to the movies!

Did you hear about
the guy who evaporated?

He will be mist.

What did the mumma cow
say to the baby cow?

'It's past-ure bedtime.'

Don't fart in an Apple store.

Because they don't
have windows.

What do you call an elephant
that nobody cares about.

Irrelephant.

What musical instrument
can you find in the bathroom?

A tuba toothpaste.

Did you hear the joke
about the hungry clock?

He went back four seconds.

What do you call a woman
with a frog on her head?

Lily.

I recently got squashed
by a load of books.

I've only got my
shelf to blame.

What do you get if a dinosaur
kicks you in the bottom?

A mega-sore-ass.

What has three legs
and four arms?

My toddler's drawing
of a snake.

How did the hamburger
introduce his girlfriend?

Meat Patty!

What do you call
James Bond in a bathtub?

Bubble 07.

What cheese do you use
to get a bear to come out
of its cave?

Cam-en-bear.

What's the best place
in the house to hide
from ghosts?

The living room.

Where does Phil Collins
record his music?

In the stu-stu-studio.

What do you get if you cross
an owl with a dog?

A growl!

A mummy covered in
chocolate and nuts has
been discovered in Egypt.

Archaeologists believe it
may be Pharaoh Rocher.

What sort of car do you buy a cat?

A Cat-illac.

My partner was getting annoyed at me singing 'Wonderwall' all day long.

She asked me to stop.

I said, 'Maybe.'

Why aren't koalas actual bears?

Because they don't meet the koalafications.

I accidentally got
tomato sauce in my eyes.

I now have Heinzsight.

David Hasselhoff has started
referring to himself as Hoff.

It's less of a hassle.

What happens when you
try talking to a cow?

Everything just goes in one ear
and out the udder.

Where do rainbows go
when they're bad?

Prism. It's a light sentence.

Knock, knock.
Who's there?
Alpaca.
Alpaca who?
Alpaca the suitcase,
you load up the car!

Knock, knock.
Who's there?
Ima.
Ima who?
I'm a panda!

Knock, knock.
Who's there?
Howard.
Howard who?
Howard you like breakfast
in bed, Mummy?

What did the sick cat say?

'I feel claw-ful.'

What do you call a cow
who just gave birth?

De-calf-inated!

My husband told me
I had to stop impersonating
a flamingo.

I had to put my foot down.

My daughter bet me $20 I couldn't
turn spaghetti into a car.

You should have seen her face
when I drove pasta.

My boss always laughed
at my jokes at work but since
the pandemic she never laughs
at them in Zoom chats.
I asked her why.

She replied,
'Because your jokes
aren't remotely funny.'

What do cows say when
they're stuck in traffic?

'Moo-ve out of my way!'

My email password
got hacked again.

That's the third time
I've had to rename the cat.

What do you call a magician
who lost his magic?

Ian.

My daughter asked me if
I had seen the dog bowl.

I said, 'No, I didn't even
know she could!'

———

What do you get if you put a duck
in a cement mixer?

Quacks in the pavement.

When should you stop
telling fart jokes?

When everyone tells you
they stink!

How does a cat make coffee?

In a purr-culator.

What did the broke frog say?

'Baroke, baroke, baroke.'

What's a duck's favourite
part of the news?

The feather forecast.

How do you know the
moon's hairless?

It spends half the
month waxing.

What cheese do
pirates love?

Ched-arrr.

What is the name of a man
with a rubber toe?

Roberto.

I rented a limo the other day for my
daughter's high school formal. It cost
$350 but it didn't come with a driver.

All that money, and nothing
to chauffeur it.

I have had to quit my job
at the cat rescue shelter.

They reduced meowers.

What did the hat say
to the scarf?

'You hang around.
I'll go on ahead.'

Lance isn't a common
name these days.

But in medieval times,
people were named
Lance a lot.

What's green and
not heavy.

Light green.

Dogs can't operate
MRI machines.

But catscan.

What do you call
a bunny with fleas?

Bugs bunny.

What do you call
a small cow?

Condensed milk.

My friend and I like to
taste new foods together.

We're taste buds.

What's red and smells
like blue paint?

Red paint.

My son told me to
put his shoes on.

I don't think they'll fit me.

I've been shopping today looking
for some camouflage clothes.

I couldn't find any!

Whenever I think of the eighties the
first thing I remember is a boom box.

But that's just a stereotype.

What did the parmesan say when it
broke up with the mozzarella?

'Sorry but I'm too mature for you.'

What do you call a man
pouring water into a glass?

Phil.

Did you hear about the
claustrophobic astronaut?

He needed a little space.

Why should you never
fight a dinosaur?

Because you'll get
Jurassicked!

Why does a duck
have a tail?

To cover up its
butt quack.

What's a koala's
favourite car?

A Furr-ari!

How many tickles does it take to tickle an octopus?

Tentacles!

Why do fish and chips always win their baseball games?

They have the best batter.

'Mum, can you give me
some personal space?'

'Well, you came out of
my personal space!'

What's the hardest part
about being a parent?

Without a shadow of
a doubt, it's the kids.

What happened when a
strawberry tried to
cross the road?

There was a traffic jam!

Why do we tell actors
to 'break a leg'?

Because every play
has a cast.

I've finally taught my dog
to fetch a glass of red wine.

He's a bordeaux collie.

And, yes, he paws it himself.

What kind of shoes
do frogs wear?

Open-toad.

Why was it so hard for the
pirate to call his mum?

Because she left the
phone off the hook.

What did the mama tomato
say to the baby tomato?

'Catch up!'

Why was Cinderella
so bad at soccer?

She kept running away
from the ball!

What do you call
a magical poo?

Poo-dini.

Why was the
hippy cat happy?

She was fe-line groovy.

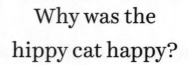

Why do cows have
hooves and not feet?

Because they lack toes!

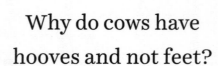

What does a pizza say when
it introduces itself to you?

'Slice to meet you.'

Why did the bee fly
with its legs crossed?

Because it couldn't
find a BP station.

What game should you
never play with a unicorn?

Leap frog!

What do you call a
sleeping pizza?

Pizzzzzzzzzzzzzza.

What do mice do
when they're home?

Mouse work!

I used to think Chewbacca
was an Ewok.

What a Wookiee mistake.

What did the cheese say
when it looked in the mirror?

'Well halloooo-meee!'

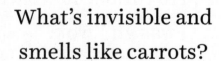

What's invisible and
smells like carrots?

Bunny farts.

Why do ducks make terrible
public speakers?

It's all the fowl language.

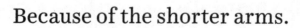

Did you know that T-shirt
is actually short for
tyrannosaurus-shirt?

Because of the shorter arms.

What made the
sausage roll?

He saw the apple
turn over.

I wrote a song
about a tortilla.

It's more of a
wrap actually.

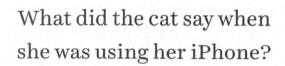

What did the cat say when
she was using her iPhone?

'Can you hear meow?'

Why did the
cheese cry?

It was having
a meltdown.

How do you know if a unicorn
has been in your house?

They leave glitter
everywhere.

What song do cats
always request when they
go to clubs?

'Mice mice baby'.

Why wouldn't
the bicycle stand
up by itself?

It was two tired.

What do you call a
bear with no ears?

A 'B'.

Why did the star
have a crush
on the sun?

It was the centre
of her universe.

What do you call
banana peel shoes?

Slippers.

Why don't mermaids
use computers?

They don't like the net!

Where do frogs go
to get their glasses?

The hoptician.

I had a hen who could
count her own eggs.

She was a mathemachicken.

Why did the alien
go to Saturn?

To go ring shopping.

What do you call a snail
driving a boat?

A snailor.

Did you hear about the red ship
and the blue ship that collided?

Both crews were marooned.

What did the buffalo say
when his son left?

'Bison.'

Do you know how a cat
likes its steak?

Rare!

What do you call a lamb
covered in chocolate?

A candy baaa.

Friends told me
I'd never get over
my obsession
with Phil Collins.

But take a look
at me now.

A bear walks into a bar
and says to the bartender:
'A champagne and . . .
a glass of rosé.

'Why the big pause?'
asks the bartender.

'I don't know, I was born
with them,' says the bear.

Why did Star Wars episodes four,
five and six come out before
one, two and three?

Because in charge of
directing, Yoda was.

What do you call
a short mother?

A minimum.

I told my cat that I'm going to
teach him to speak English.

He looked at me and said,
'Me? How?'

Who does a pharaoh
talk to when he's sad?

His mummy.

Don't use 'beef stew'
as a computer password.

It's not stroganoff.

What do you call a
magical dog?

A labra-cadabra-dor.

What colour is
the wind?

Blew.

Why do frogs want
to be rappers?

They're big into
hip hop.

How do trees access
the internet?

They log in.

When towels tell jokes . . .

They have the driest
sense of humour.

I went to the beekeeper
to get twelve bees.

She counted and gave
me thirteen.

When I said, 'Excuse me,
you gave me an extra one,'
she told me, 'That's a freebie.'

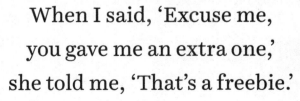

Why can you never trust
a taco with a secret?

They tend to spill the beans.

What's a foot's favourite chocolate?

Toe-blerone.

How does a panda make
pancakes in the morning?

With a pan ... duh!

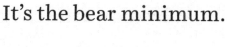

Apparently to start a zoo
you need at least two pandas,
a grizzly and three polars.

It's the bear minimum.

NASA got tired of watching
the moon orbit the Earth
for twenty-four hours.

So they called it a day.

Why didn't the cat go to
school on Wednesday?

It wasn't feline well.

What did the traffic light say
to the other traffic light?

'Don't look, I'm changing!'

How do you cut an
ocean in half?

You use a sea saw.

Did you hear about the
T-rex who sells guns?

He's a small arms dealer.

Why did the croissants take
the donuts and bagels
to Disneyland?

They thought it would be
fun for the hole family.

What do you call a herd
of giggling cows?

Laughing stock.

A shark can swim faster than me,
but I can run faster than a shark . . .

So in a triathlon, it would all come
down to who is the better cyclist.

Why didn't the toilet paper
make it across the road?

It got stuck in the crack.

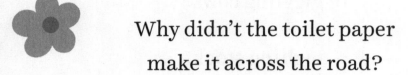

What kind of music do
fancy frogs listen to?

Hop-era!

What do you call it when a
cat is super-stylish?

Haute cat-ture.

How do you know which cow
is the best dancer?

See which one has the
best moo-ves.

What did the woman say when
she saw twin pandas?

'That bear's repeating.'

A ham sandwich walks into a bar
and orders an Aperol Spritz.

The bartender says we don't
serve food here.

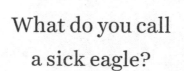

What do you call
a sick eagle?

Illegal.

Where do cow farts
come from?

The dairy air.

Knock, knock.
Who's there?
Hoot.
Hoot who?
Ha ha you talk
like an owl.

Knock, knock.
Who's there?
Annie.
Annie who?
Annie thing you can do,
Mum can do better.

Knock, knock.
Who's there?
Claws.
Claws who?
Claws the door, it's cold!

Knock, knock.
Who's there?
Cat.
Cat who?
Cat you understand!

What do you call an
espresso with a cold?

Coughee.

What did the cat
say to the cow?

'How meow
brown cow?'

What do you get when you
cross a cat and a sloth?

A slow leopard.

What do you call a polar
bear in the jungle?

Lost.

Why is a computer
so smart?

Because it listens to
its motherboard.

My husband asked me if I wanted to watch *Dr Strange* for movie night, but I said no.

I had *Stranger Things* to watch.

———

How much does a rainbow weigh?

Not much, they're actually pretty light!

———

What do you call a dinosaur fart?

A blast from the past.

Why did the mushroom get
invited to the party?

Because he was a fungi.

My friend Tony asked me
not to say his name backwards.

I said, 'Y not?'

What do you call a cheetah
with a photocopier?

A copycat.

What do you call a bear
with a bad attitude?

The bearer of bad news.

Two antennas got married.
The wedding was okay.

But the reception was incredible.

How do you have a
party in space?

You planet.

I love eye jokes.

The cornea the better.

What is Beethoven's
favourite fruit?

Banananaaaaa.

What kind of shoes
do bakers wear?

Loaf-ers.

I swallowed a dictionary today.

It gave me thesaurus throat
I've ever had.

Why did the teenage cat get
sent to his room?

He had a bad cat-titude.

I was in the supermarket
the other day when this
woman threw a block of
cheddar at me.

Outraged, I shouted,
'Well, that's not very
mature, is it?'

What's black and white
and very noisy?

A panda with a
set of drums.

What did the taco
say to the burrito?

'Where have you bean?'

Two slices of bread
got married.

The ceremony was going great,
until someone decided
to toast the bride and groom.

When does a joke become
a mum joke?

When it becomes
apparent.

I was confused when my
printer started playing music.

Until I realised the paper
was jamming.

What does a painter do
when she gets cold?

She puts on another coat.

Why did the mouse
stay inside?

Because it was raining
cats and dogs.

I'm a locksmith and
also a musician.

I recently wrote a song
which has a lovely key change.

What did the cobbler say when
a cat wandered into her shop?

Shoe!

Why do fish always
sing off-key?

You can't tuna fish.

What's the best thing about
working for a donut?

The dough!

Two goldfish in a tank.

One says to the other, 'Do you
know how to drive this thing?'

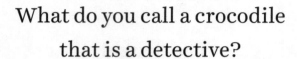

What do you call a crocodile
that is a detective?

An investi-gator.

If a group of dolphins is called
a pod, and a group of otters is
called a family, what is a group
of small children called?

Annoying.

What is a cat's
favourite magazine?

A cat-alogue.

When is a door not a door?

When it's ajar.

Why did the tomato go out
with the prune?

Because she couldn't
find a date.

What do you call it when
a snowman has a tantrum?

A meltdown.

What do you call a group
of dinosaurs who sing?

A tyranno-chorus.

If you're ever locked out of
your house, start talking to
your lock, calmly and clearly.

After all, communication is key.

What kind of shoes does
Captain Hook hate?

Crocs!

Today I was charged $10,000 for
sending my cat into space.

It was a cat-astro-fee.

What do you call a bee that
cannot make up its mind?

A maybe.

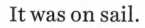

How did the pirate buy
his ship so cheaply?

It was on sail.

What type of house weighs
less than all others?

A lighthouse.

I heard a joke about chocolate
bars and it wasn't that funny.

So I just Snickered.

Why was the broom late
for the meeting?

It overswept.

What do you call a fish
wearing a tie?

So-fish-ticated.

How many birds does it take to
change a lightbulb?

Ideally three, but toucan.

The mountains aren't just funny,
they're . . . hill areas.

How does the moon
cut his hair?

Eclipse it.

What do you call
a dancing lamb?

A baaaaaa-llerina.

Almost all garden gnomes have red hats.

It's a little gnome fact.

What do you call a bee that's
having a bad hair day?

A frizz-bee.

I have a fear of speed bumps.

But I'm slowly getting over it.

Where do cats love going
on family outings?

The mew-seum.

Did you hear about the koala
that was kicked out
of the race?

She was diskoalified.

What do astronauts
drink?

Gravi-tea.

What happened when the
sloth ate the watch?

It was very time consuming.

Why is it great to have an
owl as a friend?

Because they're a hoot!

What goes 'oh oh oh'?

Santa walking backwards.

Why do potatoes make
great detectives?

Because they keep their
eyes peeled.

What makes donuts so nice?

They're very holesome.

Where do you take someone
who has been injured
in a peek-a-boo accident?

To the ICU.

My partner asked me if I could
clear the kitchen table.

I had to get a running start
but I made it.

What time did the woman
go to the dentist?

Tooth-hurty.

How do you get a baby
astronaut to sleep?

Rocket.

I once had a conversation
with a dolphin.

We just clicked.

What did the salad say
to the bouncer?

'Lettuce in.'

What is smarter than
a talking cat?

A spelling bee!

There's something
I don't like about
'DO NOT TOUCH' signs.

I just can't put my finger on it.

What is the best pasta to
make on Friday 13th?

Fettuccine afraid O.

Why did the mother
cross the road?

To get some
peace and quiet.

Why is the moon
so grumpy?

It's just going
through a phase.

What sort of shoes do
spies wear?

Sneakers.

Why didn't Han Solo
like his meal?

Because it was Chewie.

A platypus went into a bar.
She bought two glasses of rosé.

'That'll be $20 please,' said the bartender.

'Just put it on the bill,' said the platypus.

What did the cat say when
it had to stay indoors?

'Let meeee-oooout.'

Plastic surgery used to be such a taboo subject.

Now when you mention botox, nobody raises an eyebrow.

What do you get if you cross a cheetah with a burger?

Fast food.

Knock, knock.

Who's there?

Cow.

Cow who?

Cow much longer
will you put up with all
this knocking?

Knock, knock.
Who's there?
Ice cream.
Ice cream who?
ICE CREAM SO YOU
CAN HEAR ME!

⁓

Knock, knock.
Who's there?
Art.
Art who?
R2D2.

An interviewer asked me how
well I can perform under pressure.

I said I'm much better at
'Bohemian Rhapsody'.

Daughter: 'I'm hungry.'

Mum: 'Hi Hungry,
I'm Mum.'

Why did the dinosaur
take a bath?

To become ex-stinked.

How do shoes talk?

They converse.

What do you call
a sweet door?

A-dor-able.

What kind of jokes do
shoelaces tell?

Knot knot jokes.

What do you call a bear
with no teeth?

A gummy bear.

Why do bees hum?

They don't know the words.

Did you hear about the
aquatic sea mammals that
escaped from the zoo?

It was otter chaos.

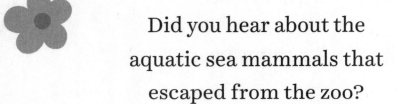

What's weirder than
seeing a cat fish?

Watching a goldfish bowl.

What kind of vehicle
does a mouse drive?

A mini-van.

You're riding a giraffe at full
speed, there is a lion right
behind you and a horse in front
of you, what do you do?

Get off the merry-go-round.

Why did the cookie cry?

Because his mother was
a wafer so long!

What are hot dogs
called in winter?

Chilly dogs.

Do you want to hear a
joke about pizza?

Never mind, it's too cheesy.

Did you hear about the
actor that fell through
the floorboards?

He was going through
a stage.

What do you call a
mermaid on a roof?

Ariel.

'Waiter, waiter do you
have frog legs?'

'No, I always walk this way.'

The past, present and
future walk into a bar.

It was intense.

I went to the zoo the other day.
There was only one dog there.

It was a shih tzu!

I'd like to have kids one day . . .

But I don't think I could
cope with them longer
than that.

My friend told me
he doesn't like milk.

How dairy.

What do you call a can
opener that doesn't work?

A can't opener.

Have you heard about the movie
called *Constipation*?

It hasn't come out yet!

How do you tell the difference between
an alligator and a crocodile?

You will see one later and
one in a while.

What month are
goats born in?

Maaaaay.

Why did the tomato blush?

Because it saw the salad
dressing.

What do you give
a sick bird?

Tweet-meant!

What do you call a mum with
sausages on her head?

Barbie.

When the dog sat on the sandpaper,
what did he say?

'Ruff! Ruff!'

Why don't oysters donate to charity?

Because they are shellfish.

What do you call a train
carrying bubble gum?

A chew-chew train.

How does a mouse feel
after taking a shower?

Squeaky clean.

Waiter: 'Do you want
any dessert?'

Teddy Bear: 'No thanks,
I'm stuffed.'

Why did the apple run away?

Because the banana split.

What happens before
it rains chocolate?

It sprinkles.

Last night it was raining
cats and dogs.

I stepped in a poodle.

What do you call a
speedy seamstress?

Taylor Swift.

Why did the platypus
cross the road?

To show the possum
it could be done.

I don't trust stairs.

They are always up
to something.

What happened when the
frog's car broke down?

He jump-started it.

Why can't you tell an egg a joke?

Because it will crack up.

What's a dog's favourite
kind of pizza?

Pup-eroni.

My husband rearranged the
labels on the spice rack.

I haven't confronted him yet
but the thyme is cumin.

I'm telling people about the benefits of dried grapes.

It's all about raisin awareness.

What do you call a T-rex with a bloody knee?

A dino-sore.

What hides in a bakery
at Christmas?

A mince spy.

Did you hear about the
restaurant on the moon?

It's got great food but
no atmosphere.

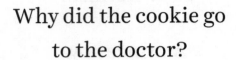

Why did the cookie go
to the doctor?

Because she felt
crummy.

What did the nacho
say to the taco?

'I'm nacho friend.'

I've chicken-proofed
my lawn.

It's impeccable.

What made the cat
upgrade her phone?

She wanted to finally
get pawtrait mode.

'Waiter, will my
pizza be long?'

'No madam, it will
be round!'

How do you make
a milk shake?

Give it a good scare.

What cheese is
made backwards?

Edam.

Why do fish avoid
the computer?

So they don't get caught
on the internet.

What did the mayonnaise
say to the fridge?

'Close the door, I'm dressing.'

What did the dalmatian
say after lunch?

'That hit the spot.'

How do chickens bake a cake?

From scratch.

What do you call an
American bee?

A USB.

What is the best way to get in touch with a fish?

Drop it a line.

Why did the kids give
their mum a blanket
for Mother's Day?

Because they thought
she was the coolest mum.

Did you hear about
the party at the zoo?

It was panda-monium.

What's delicious
and goes 'meow'?

A bis-cat.

I spent my entire life
savings on pasta.

It was worth every penne.

What do you call a paper
airplane that doesn't fly?

Stationary.

How did Darth Vader
know what Luke got
him for Christmas?

He felt his presents.

When is a car not a car?

When it turns into
a driveway.

Why are frogs
always happy?

Because they eat
whatever bugs them.

What do cows read
in the morning?

The moos paper.

I love the way the
Earth rotates.

It really makes my day.

What is an owl's
favourite subject?

Owl-gebra.

Why don't giraffes
make good pets?

They're too high
maintenance.

What do you call a
famous hedgehog?

Hegendary.

How do you make
a mouse smile?

Say 'cheese'!

How do cows clean
their apartments?

With a Hoove-r.

Why can't a leopard hide?

Because he's always spotted.

What kind of cars
do eggs drive?

Yolkswagens.

What do you call a horse
with insomnia?

A nightmare.

What did the blanket say
when it fell off the bed?

'Oh sheet!'

I took my dog to the beach
today and noticed he
floats very well.

He's a very good buoy.

Why do zebras have stripes?

Because they don't want
to be spotted.

What do you call a
man who claps
at Christmas?

Santapplause!

How do you make
a sausage roll?

Push it down
the hill.

What is an astronaut's
favourite part of
the keyboard?

The space bar.

Why don't bananas snore?

Because they don't want to
wake up the rest of the bunch.

Did you get the joke
about the roof?

Don't worry, it was
over your head.

What do you call a dinosaur
who is a noisy sleeper?

A tyranno-snorus.

How much room do
fungi need to grow?

As mushroom
as possible.

Why did the M&M
go to university?

Because she wanted
to be a Smartie.

Why is a baby chicken
less expensive than
an adult one?

Because it's a
little cheeper.

What can one parrot do?

Not as much as toucan.

Why couldn't the pony
sing a lullaby?

It was a little horse.

How do poets say hello?

'Hey, haven't
we metaphor?'

What do frogs
do with paper?

Rip it!

What sort of photos
do fairies take?

Elfies!

I watched a documentary
last night about how
pickles are made.

It was jarring.

What did one toilet say
to the other?

'You look a bit flushed.'

How do you tell a frog to
get into your car?

'Hop in!'

What is the most popular
fish in the ocean?

A starfish!

What do you give a
sausage dog with a fever?

Mustard—it's the best
thing for a hot dog!

When do ducks
usually wake up?

At the quack of dawn!

Why is it hard to have a
conversation with a goat?

They always butt in!

Why shouldn't you write
a book on penguins?

Because writing a book on
paper is much easier!

What car does a
snake drive?

An ana-Honda!

What do you call a group of killer
whales playing instruments?

An orca-stra.

What's a panda's favourite
thing to draw?

Self paw-traits.

Why did the banana
go to the doctor?

It wasn't peeling well.

Why doesn't James Bond
fart in bed?

Because it would
blow his cover.

Despite space being
a vacuum . . .

Mars is really dusty.

What do sharks have
on their toast?

Mermalaid!

I taught my pet wolf
how to meditate.

Now she's an aware wolf.

What is an egg's least
favourite day of the week?

Fry-day.

What's the difference between
a cat and a comma?

A cat has claws at the end of its paws.
A comma is a pause at the end of a clause.

Can February march?

No, but April may.

Where does an astronaut
dock her spacecraft?

At a parking meteor.

Knock, knock.
Who's there?
Figs.
Figs who?
Figs the doorbell,
it's not working.

Knock, knock.
Who's there?
Woo.
Woo who?
Glad you're excited too!

Knock, knock.
Who's there?
Justin.
Justin who?
Justin time for dinner.

Knock, knock.
Who's there?
Donut.
Donut who?
Donut forget to
close the door!

What did the hamburger
say to the pickle?

'You're dill-icious.'

Coles has a new rule that when you
buy carrots and cabbage you
must buy mayonnaise.

It's called Coles-law.

I went to the zoo and saw
a baguette in a cage.

It was bread in captivity.

What did the mama shark
say to the teen shark?

'Don't be sharkastic with me!'

Why did the chicken
go to the gym?

To build up its pecs.

Where do sharks
go on holidays?

Finland.

What do sheep do
on a sunny day?

They have a baa-baa-que!

Why are sport stadiums
always so cool?

They are filled with fans.

What do sloths like to read?

Snooze-papers.

Where do lions sell
their unwanted stuff?

At a jungle sale!

How do you know if a car
belongs to a witch?

It goes *brrroom brrroom*.

Which dinosaur knew
the most words?

The thesaurus!

What do you call a pig
who steals stuff?

A hamburglar!

Why was the
shark blushing?

It saw the
ocean's bottom.

What's an alligator's
favourite card game?

Snap!

What do you call
a sleeping bull?

A bulldozer!

What is a prickly pear?

Two hedgehogs!

Why do owls get
invited to parties?

Because they're a hoot!

What did the panda
give her mum?

A bear hug.

What's spotted and goes
round and round?

A cheetah in a
revolving door.

What did one ocean say
to the other ocean?

Nothing, it just waved.

What kind of jewellery
do rabbits wear?

Fourteen-carrot gold.

How do snails fight?

They slug it out.

What do you call a beehive
without an exit?

Unbelievable.

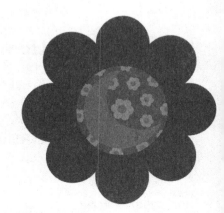

Why shouldn't you write
with a broken pencil?

It's pointless.

How do you stop a bull
from charging?

Cancel its credit card.

What do sea
monsters eat?

Fish and ships.

What do you call a
boring dinosaur?

A dino-snore.

What has more
lives than a cat?

A frog, because it
croaks every day.

What do you call a row of
rabbits hopping away?

A receding hare line.

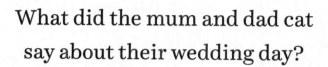

What did the mum and dad cat
say about their wedding day?

'It was unfurgettable.'

I grilled a chicken for over
two hours last night.

She still wouldn't tell me why
she crossed the road.

Five ants rented a house
with five other ants.

Now they're tenants.

What kinds of magazines
do cows read?

Cattle-logs.

I always keep a
guitar in my car.

It's good for traffic jams.

My favourite teacher at
school was Mrs Turtle.

Weird name, but she
tortoise well.

Where do you find
a Himalayan cat?

You'll find him-a-lay-in
on the couch.

—

I put my car into reverse.

Aaaah, I thought,
this takes me back.

What did the elevator
say when it sneezed?

'I think I'm coming
down with something.'

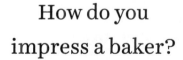
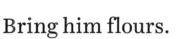

How do you
impress a baker?

Bring him flours.

What do you get if you mix
ducks with firecrackers?

Firequackers!

Why do elephants have
so many wrinkles?

Because they don't fit
on an ironing board.

What smells like fish but is
invisible?

Penguin farts.

Mum's spaghetti got in the
Guinness Book of Records.

I hope she cleans the pages.

What do you call a man
with gravy and potatoes
on his head?

Stew.

Why did the T-rex eat raw meat?

Because its itty-bitty arms
couldn't work the oven.

How does an avocado
fairytale end?

Happily avo after.

What do stars read
before bed?

Comet books.

What did the drummer
name his twin daughters?

Anna one, Anna two.

What do you call a camel
that lost his humps?

Humphrey.

What did the frog say after
he visited the theatre?

'It was ribbiting.'

Today was my son's fourth birthday.
I didn't recognise him at first.

I had never seen him be four.

A weasel walks into a bar.
The bartender says,
'What can I get you?'

'Pop,' goes the weasel.

What did the alien
say to the cat?

'Take me to your litter.'

I got fired from my last job at
the orange juice factory.

They said I couldn't
concentrate.

Never believe an atom.

They make up everything.

What's a frog's favourite drink?

Croak-a-cola!

What did the shy
pebble say?

'I wish I was a
little boulder.'

Where do cows get
their medicine?

The farmacy!

What do you get if you cross
a cheetah with a burger?

Fast food!

What do you call
an angry pig?

Disgruntled.

I got a new haircut a
couple of days ago.

I wasn't sure at first.

But it's growing on me.

My grandad used to say, 'As one door closes another one opens.'

Great guy.

Terrible carpenter.

What did the moon say to Saturn?

'Give me a ring sometime!'

Why do bees have
sticky hair?

Because they use
honeycombs.

What do you call a
detective who accidentally
solves the case?

Sheer-luck Holmes.

Why was the pig
covered in ink?

Because it lived in a pen.

Why do cows have bells?

Because their horns
don't work.

Do you know the guy
who invented knock knock?

He won the Nobel, because
there was no bell on the door!

What sort of dinosaur
has the cleanest teeth?

A Flossiraptor.

Why is Billy Joel's washing
still soaking wet?

He didn't start the dryer.

What is worse than
raining cats and dogs?

Hailing taxis.

What does a secret agent
do at bedtime?

She goes undercover.

My husband fainted and fell onto
the luggage carousel at the airport.

Thankfully, he came around.

What's yellow and goes
round and around?

A banana in a
washing machine.

What do polar bears
eat for lunch?

Ice-burgers!

Knock, knock.

Who's there?

Annie.

Annie who?

Annie one know how to get a sloth to come down from a tree?

Knock, knock.
Who's there?
Luke.
Luke who?
Luke through the
keyhole to see.

Knock, knock.
Who's there?
Lettuce.
Lettuce who?
Lettuce in already.

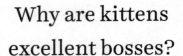

Why are kittens
excellent bosses?

They have great littership.

Why was the cutlery
stuck together?

It had been spooning.

What do you call an
encyclopaedia in the freezer?

Cold, hard facts.

What did the fish say when
it ran into the wall?

'Dam.'

Why don't farts do
well at school?

They get expelled!

What did the frog say
when he went to the library?

'Reddit! Reddit! Reddit!'

Roses are red,

Violets are blue.

My mum jokes

Are funnier than you.

I'm the best at
sleeping.

I can do it with
my eyes closed.

Why did the cow want to get
in the rocket ship?

He wanted to go to
udder space.

What does garlic do
when it gets hot?

It removes its cloves.

Why did Adele
cross the road?

To say 'hello' from
the other side.

What do you call a
clock on the moon?

A lunar-tick!

Why do bananas have to wear sunscreen?

Because they peel.

What did the tortoise say when she was dating the sloth?

'Let's taake it sloooooooow.'

Why couldn't the
pirate play cards?

Because he was sitting
on the deck!

What do you call a
pig that does karate?

A pork chop.

What sound do porcupines
make when they kiss?

Ouch!

What are bears
without bees?

Ears!

What do you get when
you cross a lemon
and a cat?

A sour puss.

What is a cat's
favourite movie?

The Sound of Mew-sic.

Why did the
astronaut swear?

He stubbed
his Pluto.

What do you sing at a
snowman's birthday party?

Freeze a jolly good fellow.

Why don't skeletons
fart in public?

Because they haven't got the guts.

Where do dogs
park their cars?

In the barking lot.

What's orange and
sounds like 'parrot'?

A carrot!

I walked down the street
dressed as a screwdriver.

I turned a few heads.

What do pandas drink?

Bambooze.

How do you keep baby cows quiet,
so their mums can sleep late?

Use the moooooote button.

Why was the cat so upset?

Because she was in a bad mewd.

What sort of chocolate
can you buy at the airport?

Plane chocolate.

What did the Earth tease
the moon about?

Having no life!

What do reindeers hang
on their Christmas trees?

Horn-aments!

What do you call
twin dinosaurs?

Pair-odactyls.

How did the oyster manage
to hide from the fish?

Clam-ouflage!

Why do cats always
get their way?

They are very
purr-suasive.

Child: 'What's for dinner?'

Mum: 'Food.'

Child: 'What kind?'

Mum: 'The kind you eat.'

Why don't you trust Elsa
to hold your balloon?

Because she will
'Let it go!'

What do dogs eat
at the movies?

Pup-corn.

What happens when a frog's car breaks down?

It gets toad.

Why is Peter Pan always flying?

He neverlands.

What do you call an
alligator in a vest?

An in-vest-igator.

What's black and white,
black and white, and
black and white?

A panda bear rolling down a hill.

What kind of shows
do cows like best?

Moo-sicals.

What's a cat's favourite
sushi roll?

Tempurrra.

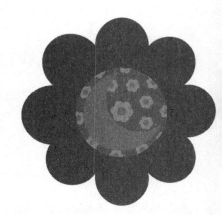

What did the cat wearing
a bird disguise say?

'Me-owl.'

What is a geologist's
favourite music genre?

Rock!

Why don't dinosaurs
make good pets?

Because they're dead.

What do you call a dog
in a submarine?

A subwoofer.

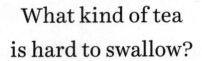

What kind of tea
is hard to swallow?

Reality.

What do you call
a mum who can't draw?

Tracy.

What do horses say
when they fall?

'Help, I've fallen and
I can't giddy up.'

What did the hermit crabs
do on Mother's Day?

They shell-a-brated their mum!

'After a long day, my favourite thing is to think of something for dinner that everyone will eat,' said no mother ever.

Why are ghosts the worst liars?

You can see right through them.

What did the monkey say
when she caught her tail in
the revolving door?

'It won't be long now.'

Have you heard the one about
the corduroy pillow?

It's making headlines.

Did you hear about the hyena
who drank a litre of gravy?

He was a laughing stock!

What's it called when you
lend money to a bison?

A buffa-loan.

What do calendars eat?

Dates.

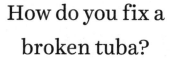

How do you fix a
broken tuba?

With a tuba glue.

What do you call it when a
dinosaur crashes his car?

Tyrannosaurus Wrecks.

What does a ghost wear
when it's raining outside.

Booooooooots.

Why do milking stools
only have three legs?

Because the cows
got the udder.

Which side of a cheetah
has the most spots?

The outside.

Knock, knock.
Who's there?
Isabelle.
Isabelle who?
Isabelle working,
or should I
keep knocking?

Knock, knock.

Who's there?

Dozen.

Dozen who?

Dozen anyone want
to let me in.

What did the sushi
say to the bee?

'Wasabi!'

What did the grape say after
the elephant sat on it?

Nothing, it just let out
a little whine.

I'm not a fan
of elevator music.

It's bad on so
many levels.

What do you call a rabbit
that is really cool?

A hip hopper.

Why does it take pirates
so long to learn
the alphabet?

Because they can
spend years at C!

My husband: 'Why don't you
stop telling crap mum jokes
and write a book instead?'

Me: 'That's . . . a novel idea.'